READING ABOUT

Rain or Shine

By Jim Pipe

Aladdin/Watts
London • Sydney

Weather

What is the weather today?

Some days it rains.

Some days the sun shines.

Some days both happen!

Gina's mum likes rain *and* shine.
Her plants need both to grow.

Hot and cold

What is the weather?

Some days are hot. Gina wears shorts and a shirt. She wishes she was at the beach!

Some days are cold. Gina wears lots of clothes. Everything is icy.

Sun

What is the weather?

It is sunny. Gina and Ali
like to play in the sun.

Gina's cat likes the sun, too.

But her dog likes the shade.

It pants to keep cool.

Clouds

What is the weather?

It is cloudy. There are fluffy white clouds on sunny days. Grey clouds can bring rain.

Gina and Ali look for shapes in the clouds.
What shapes can you see?

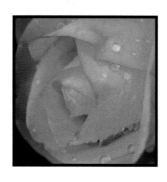

Rain

What is the weather?

It is raining. First there are a few small drops. Then it pours. Ali and Gina love puddles!

Some people use an umbrella
in the rain.
It keeps them dry!

Wind

What is the weather?

It is windy. The wind blows Gina and Ali's boat across the water.

You can feel the wind in your hair.

You can hear it in the trees.

Can you see the wind?

Storm

What is the weather?

There is a storm. The wind blows hard. The rain pours and pours.

A big storm can blow down trees.
Lots of rain can flood the streets.

Thunder and lightning

What is the weather?

It is a thunderstorm.

The thunder goes BOOM!

Lightning flashes across the sky.

Gina loves the storm, but the noise scares her dog.

Snow

What is the weather?

It is snowing. It is very cold outside. Gina and Ali play on their sledge.

A big snowstorm is called a blizzard.
Some cars get stuck in the snow.

Rainbow

What is the weather?

Sometimes it rains *and* shines.

The sun shines through the rain and makes a beautiful rainbow in the sky.

Here are some kinds of weather.

Sunny

Windy

Rainy

Snow

Cloudy

Here are some weather words.

Lightning

Hot

Puddle

Umbrella

Can you write a story
with these words?

Do you know?

Some storms are very big.

Some winds spin very fast.

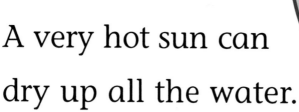

A very hot sun can dry up all the water.